SERIOUSLY WEIRD TRUE STORIES

Herbie Brennan

Illustrated by
David Wyatt

Scholastic Children's Books,
Commonwealth House, 1–19 New Oxford Street
London WC1A 1NU, UK

A division of Scholastic Ltd
London ~ New York ~ Toronto ~ Sydney ~ Auckland

Published in the UK by Scholastic Ltd, 1997

Text copyright © Herbie Brennan, 1997
Illustrations copyright © David Wyatt, 1997

ISBN 0 590 13973 8

Typeset by Rapid Reprographics Ltd
Printed by Cox & Wyman Ltd, Reading, Berks

10 9 8 7 6 5 4 3 2 1

The right of Herbie Brennan and David Wyatt to be identified as the author
and illustrator of this work respectively has been asserted by them in
accordance with the Copyright, Designs and Patents Act, 1988.

CONTENTS

Introduction 5

The Man Who Murdered Himself 9

The Green Children of Woolpit 17

Tomorrow will be Froggy: Weird Weather Facts 27

Zzzzzz 35

Dream of Death 43

The Chinese Dragon 55

A Hitch in Time 69

Impossible Antique 79

Stone Me! Weird Stone Circle Facts 89

The Incredible Plum Pudding Weirdness 93

The Boy from Nowhere 101

Afterword 111

Introduction

Life can get seriously weird. Just how weird you're about to find out.

During April, 1990, a 79-year-old woman died in Essen, Germany, when an Airedale terrier fell on her head.

Four years later, a New Zealand farmer died when a giant pumpkin fell on his.

Neither was related to the crew of the rowing boat which was capsized by a falling cow off the Pacific coast of the former Soviet Union in 1990.

In 1982, a gunman in Phoenix, Arizona, went out into the desert and started to use a giant saguaro cactus for target practice, despite the fact that it was (and is) an endangered species. The upper section of the plant broke off, fell on top of him and speared him to death with its spines.

If that doesn't sound too weird, then how do you feel about the exploding cat, Peppi, who detonated without explanation in the Anmer Lodge Old Folks Home in London?

Or the 26,000 chickens (all fortunately dead at the time) that exploded on Larry Mohler's ranch in Oregon? Or the 82-year-old patient of Nottingham Hospital who exploded in 1988 while he was having surgery?

Weirdness is nothing new in human history. In 234 BC three moons were reported in the sky over Rimini. Eleven years later they appeared again "in many portions of Italy".

Pliny, the Roman historian, mentions that they were back again the following year, 222 BC, while another year later they turned up for a second time over Rimini. There were phantom ships in the sky and apparitions of men in gleaming clothing in 218 BC.

The following year came reports of a shrunken sun fighting with the moon, the sky catching fire over Capua, a crack in the sky over Falerii, two moons rising (during daytime) over Caperne, while one fell "in a shower of rain", again at Capua.

You may suspect the Ancient Romans didn't know what they were looking at. But if they weren't looking at actual suns and moons, they were certainly looking at something seriously weird.

With this sort of history, it's no surprise that humanity is still seriously weird today. There are, for example, scientists who believe we weave in and out of different universes all the time.

But if you don't think any of this is very weird, read on. There's evidence that all the stories in this book are true.

Although you'll probably never believe it.

The Man Who Murdered Himself

Our first case study happened only a few years ago in the United States. It's a tragic tale, but so weird you'll never hear the like of it again.

Chicago, USA, 1992

In 1992, a man flung himself from the roof of a 26-storey high-rise apartment building in Chicago.

As he was passing the fourteenth floor, a gunshot from one of the apartments caught him in the head and killed him instantly.

Police investigating the shooting had an interesting problem: was the crime suicide or murder? It wasn't easy to decide. There were a lot of complications.

The first was that, unknown to the man, a firm of window cleaners had set up safety netting at the level of the twelfth floor. This netting was designed to catch anybody who fell from a ledge while cleaning windows. But it was wide enough to catch anyone falling from the roof.

So the man would not have died from the fall.

Since he did die from the gunshot wound, it looked as if the case had to be murder. The question was, who did it?

When the police investigated, they found that the apartment from which the gunshot had come belonged to an elderly couple.

On the afternoon in question they had been having a fight. In the course of this fight, the husband took a gun from a desk drawer, aimed it at his wife and fired.

The shot missed the woman, but passed through the window and killed the man attempting to commit suicide outside. It looked as if the police had found their murderer.

Or had they?

The man who pulled the trigger claimed he thought the gun was empty. He said he often fought with his wife and was in the habit of threatening her with an empty gun.

The police didn't believe this. But when they talked to the wife, she said it was true. They were always fighting. Her husband was always threatening to shoot her. But the gun was never ever loaded. The whole thing was just a silly game between them.

Neither she nor her husband had the least idea how the gun came to be loaded this one time.

The police decided to forget about charging anybody for the moment and started to look into another important question:

Who loaded the gun?

The answer seemed to be the couple's teenage son. And the loading of the gun was not an innocent mistake. The boy was due to inherit a substantial sum of money on his mother's death. He knew about his father's habit of firing the empty gun at the mother when they argued. So he secretly loaded the gun and waited for his father to shoot her.

But the parents didn't fight for several weeks. Their son became depressed about money and eventually decided to commit suicide.

11

He flung himself off the roof of the apartment building where he lived and was shot by the gun he had loaded as he passed his parents' apartment on the fourteenth floor.

• Although the police decided not to charge the boy's father, he could have faced several possible charges, among them:
Accidental killing of his son.
Abusive behaviour.
Causing a breach of the peace.
Unlawful discharge of a firearm.
Possession of an unlicensed handgun.

• If the gunshot hadn't killed the boy, but only wounded him, he too could have faced a number of charges including:
Attempted murder of his mother.
Attempted suicide.
Reckless endangerment of property, namely a window cleaner's safety net.

• The Chicago police detective in charge of the investigation now makes his living by giving talks about the case.

1. In the winter of 1989, at a housing estate in Barnsley, Yorkshire, four concrete lamp-posts were found uprooted during a single night. Residents awoke next morning to find the posts had not been snapped off – as might be expected if they'd been struck by a car – but literally pulled up out of their foundations by something very tall and very, very strong.

2. In 1987, there was an outbreak of bridge theft. Two cases occurred in Wales where a wooden footbridge over the River Penrhos disappeared less than a month after it was built. Undaunted, the local council replaced it with a six-metre steel structure weighing many tons. That was promptly nicked as well. It's not known whether there was any connection between the Welsh thefts and that of a fifty-metre long iron bridge in Uruguay which went missing at about the same time.

3. There was no sign of a break-in at the strong room of Kennedy Airport, New York, on 12 April, 1967, despite the fact that $143,000 was missing. The thieves had got in – and out – through a double-locked steel door without alerting the armed guards or leaving any indication of how they made their entry.

4. In 1969 a man walked into a bank in Portland, Oregon, and showed the teller a piece of paper on which he'd written: *This is a hold-up. I've got a gun.*

The robber then put the paper on the counter, took out a pen and added laboriously: *Put the money in a paper bag.*

He pushed the paper underneath the grille and waited. The cashier picked it up, read it carefully, then took out a pen of his own and scrawled across the bottom: *I don't have a paper bag.*

He pushed it back underneath the grille. The robber read it and left.

5. In 1980, a robber walked into a Liverpool jeweller's shop brandishing a weapon and announcing a stick-up. Nobody took him seriously because they recognized the weapon as a popgun due to the bright red plastic cork the man had forgotten to remove from the muzzle.

6. Half an ear was stolen from an Arizona woman during the night of 15 September, 1985. This painful theft was all the more mysterious since there was no sign of a break-in.

7. A six-foot mugger threatened a five-foot tall 74-year-old grandmother in Chichester Cathedral, but ran away screaming when she grabbed his wrist.

8. In November 1933, a French burglar attempted to rob a house while wearing a full suit of armour. He made so much noise that the owner woke up and pushed a sideboard over on him. The move not only ensured the burglar's capture, but damaged the armour so badly that it proved impossible to get off. For his first day in custody, the man had to be fed through his visor while waiting for a blacksmith to cut him out.

9. In 1978, a burglar fell into a chip fryer while robbing a Chinese restaurant in Devon. Half blinded by congealing grease, he walked into the arms of a policeman while trying to find his way out.

10. A ghost set off a burglar alarm in the Norfolk home of Kenneth Broadhead in 1974. Nothing was missing, but there was a trail of footprints – all made by a single shoe – which ended against a brick wall. Local people believed the house was haunted by a one-legged Jesuit.

11. Three thieves raided the Billericay Post Office, Essex, in 1971, despite the fact it had been closed for twelve years.

12. It now costs so much to keep a prisoner in jail that some experts believe it would be cheaper to *pay* criminals to keep on the straight and narrow. One has suggested a flat-rate pension which would be stopped if a crime was committed.

The Green Children of Woolpit

In the Suffolk village of Woolpit you can still hear about a very weird occurrence in the district during the Dark Ages. Here it is.

Suffolk, England, about 1150

During the reign of King Stephen, it was common practice to dig pits to catch the wolves that often attacked livestock.

One morning, farm workers checking the wolf traps that ringed the Suffolk village of Woolpit found they had caught not wolves but two young children, a boy and a girl.

They were both green.

They dressed in green. They had green skin. Their hair was green.

The children could talk, but not in any language the farm workers understood. Not knowing what else to do with their find, the men took the children to the castle of Sir Richard de Calne, the local squire.

Sir Richard examined the children with astonishment, decided they must be hungry as well as strange, and ordered them fed.

But his staff could not persuade them to eat. They both

looked as if they could do with a good meal, yet refused everything that was placed before them.

Eventually one of the cooks got lucky and tried them on green beans. Perhaps because of the familiar colour, the children ate them.

They survived on beans for several days, but were gradually persuaded to add other foods to their diet until after a month or so they were eating normally.

Despite this, the boy pined away and died. His sister remained healthy. Sir Richard's staff actually succeeded in teaching her to speak English.

Once the girl could make herself understood, she told a strange story.

She and her brother, she said, had been born and had grown up in a "Christian land" named St Martins.

It was a strange country. Everything was green: trees, plants, grass, animals, houses, even people. There was no sun in the land – it was bathed in perpetual twilight.

But the children could see a land of light across a river near their home.

The boy and girl, it seemed, were the children of a shepherd and often tended his flocks. While doing so, they were caught up by a whirlwind and dropped near the village of Woolpit.

The girl later changed this story.

According to her second version, she and her brother heard bells while tending the flock.

They followed the sound and discovered an underground passageway. After some hesitation they entered. Fumbling through the darkness, they followed the passage until it emerged again above ground.

But now they were in a different world, a world of clear

skies and bright light. They were exploring when they fell into the wolf pit where they were found.

• The story of the green children is given in two separate sources – the writings of the Mediaeval historians William of Newburgh and Ralph of Coggeshall.

• The girl lost her green colouring and grew up to marry a man from King's Lynn.

• Thetford Forest, to the north-west of Woolpit, is the site of ancient Stone Age flint mines, which may have been the underground passages the children followed.

• An illness called green chlorosis can turn your skin green. The disease is a form of anaemia that affects the cells of the blood and may be made worse by the wrong sort of diet. Since the youngsters refused normal food after they were found, it's quite likely they hadn't been eating properly for quite a long time before then.

• Some experts believe the popular fairy tale, The Babes in the Wood, was based on the story of the green children at Woolpit. Early forms of the story say that the babes, a boy and a girl, were poisoned with arsenic before being abandoned in Thetford Forest. Arsenic poisoning can also sometimes turn skin green.

• There's some suggestion that the strange language spoken by the children wasn't a different language at all, but just English with a particularly thick accent – so thick nobody in Woolpit could understand it.

1. By the age of five, in 1990, Sher Ali of Bangladesh had managed to grow a ten-centimetre long beard. His father, a former saucepan salesman, took him around country fairs where he was exhibited as a holy boy. People paid to touch him, believing he had healing powers. Sher Ali isn't unique. There have been a number of hairy children born all over the world. Sometimes the hairiness gets so extreme it covers the entire body and face.

2. In 1939, a black couple, Mr and Mrs Herbert Strong from North Carolina, USA, gave birth to twins, a boy and a girl. The girl was black like her parents, but the boy was white.

3. Andrew Vandal was born in Virginia, USA, in 1984 without a brain. He had a rare condition known as hydrancephaly, which left his skull full of nothing except fluid. Doctors who attended the birth were convinced he would die, but he didn't. Andrew survived to be adopted by a nurse from Connecticut who describes him as a "glowing, outgoing, bubbly personality". Mrs Vandal has two other children with the same condition. One of them, a girl, was still going strong at the age of twelve without a brain. In 1982, ITV broadcast a progamme which included the case history of a boy named Stephen who managed five 'O'

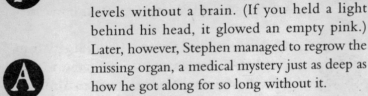

levels without a brain. (If you held a light behind his head, it glowed an empty pink.) Later, however, Stephen managed to regrow the missing organ, a medical mystery just as deep as how he got along for so long without it.

4. Horror writer Stephen King once published a book called *Firestarter* about a child who could set things alight by concentrating on them. Before the age of ten, an Italian schoolboy, Benedetto Supino, discovered he could do it for real. In 1982, he was reading a comic in a dentist's waiting room when it burst into flames. From that point on, just about everything he touched was scorched – and even things he only looked at could catch fire. The talent had its drawbacks. One morning he woke to find his bedclothes on fire and was himself quite badly burned. Benedetto also seems to influence electrical equipment, which tends to break down when he's about. Doctors who examined him at the Tivoli Social Medical Centre pronounced him "perfectly normal".

5. Nine-year-old Mark Bowker lost the tip of his finger when he caught his hand in a door at his school in Oxfordshire. To the astonishment of doctors, he then grew a new one. The ability to regrow chopped-off bits of your body is quite common in babies, but disappears around the age of three. Certain lizards are a lot better at this than humans of any age – they can

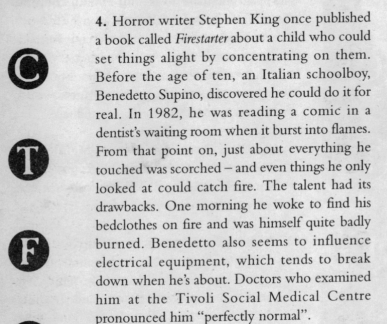

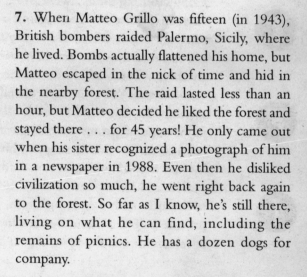

regenerate whole limbs in a matter of weeks.

6. Matanet, an eleven-year-old girl from Azerbaijan, somehow managed to swallow a 64 cm poisonous Caucasian cat snake in her sleep. She woke up choking one morning in August, 1987, and was taken to the Children's Clinic at Baku where, after drinking three and a half pints of salt water, she brought up the snake again. Matanet went home an hour later none the worse for wear. I can find no record of what happened to the snake.

7. When Matteo Grillo was fifteen (in 1943), British bombers raided Palermo, Sicily, where he lived. Bombs actually flattened his home, but Matteo escaped in the nick of time and hid in the nearby forest. The raid lasted less than an hour, but Matteo decided he liked the forest and stayed there . . . for 45 years! He only came out when his sister recognized a photograph of him in a newspaper in 1988. Even then he disliked civilization so much, he went right back again to the forest. So far as I know, he's still there, living on what he can find, including the remains of picnics. He has a dozen dogs for company.

8. In 1977, eight-year-old Julian Fabricus, of Worcester, South Africa, complained of an itch in his left eye. An optical specialist, Dr Cornelius Kooy, discovered a 4mm-long plant –

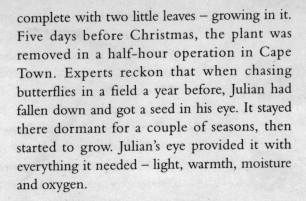

complete with two little leaves – growing in it. Five days before Christmas, the plant was removed in a half-hour operation in Cape Town. Experts reckon that when chasing butterflies in a field a year before, Julian had fallen down and got a seed in his eye. It stayed there dormant for a couple of seasons, then started to grow. Julian's eye provided it with everything it needed – light, warmth, moisture and oxygen.

9. At the age of nine, Claire Booth from Congleton, Cheshire, went deaf. Three years later she banged her head against a wall during a heated argument with her mother and her hearing returned. She may have been practising an ancient form of Hindu medicine without even knowing it. A British traveller in Delhi tells how he consulted a traditional practitioner in the hope of getting something for a streaming head cold. The doctor strapped him into what looked like an upright iron bedstead, then pulled a hidden lever. The bedstead fell backwards with a hideous crash, scaring the patient half to death. But when the doctor released him, the shock had cured his cold.

10. Romulus and Remus, the two legendary founders of Rome, were supposed to have been raised by a wolf sometime prior to 753 BC. More than two thousand years later, in 1973, the Italian authorities discovered another child who seems to have been brought up the same way. Named Rocco after an area of the Abruzzi mountains where he was found, the boy made wolf-like noises and bit anybody who went near him.

11. In November 1967, in Rosenheim, Germany, the lighting system in the office of lawyer Sigmund Adam began to go wrong. He ordered a special meter installed that showed peculiar surges in the electrical current.

The local electrical company tried installing a direct cable. The lights still malfunctioned. Herr Adam then had his own generator put in and changed all his strip lights for ordinary bulbs. It made no difference. He was still wondering what to do when his phone bill arrived. It was gigantic.

Technicians installed a special device that traced every outgoing call. To their astonishment, it showed someone was dialling the speaking clock for hours on end, four, five and even six times a minute. But this was impossible. It took a minimum of seven seconds to make the connection.

Professor Hans Bender of Freiburg, one of Europe's leading ghost hunters, discovered a lot more was going on than people realized. Lights would swing for no apparent reason, pictures turned on the wall and a heavy filing cabinet was moved by unseen hands.

Everything that happened – and more – was

associated with a teenage girl, Anne-Marie Schaberl, who had joined the company two years previously. When she walked along the corridor, the overhead lights would begin to swing back and forth and the mysterious surges of current occurred only when she was in the building.

With equipment still going wrong all around her, Herr Adam fired the girl. She took a job in another office where more trouble broke out. When she went ten-pin bowling with her fiancé the electronic equipment ceased to function properly. She took a mill job, but left when a machinery malfunction led to the death of a co-worker.

Tomorrow will be Froggy:
Weird Weather Facts

People love to talk about the weather . . . and sometimes they have a lot to talk about. Frogs and fish are the most common weird rains, but the history books – not to mention modern day accounts – all show just about anything can come pelting from the sky. Check out this special Fact File for just a very few dated sightings world-wide.

1. On 24 October, 1987, the *Daily Mirror* published the world's weirdest weather report – a story about a heavy downpour of pink frogs.

Residents of Stroud in Gloucestershire were pelted by the little creatures during a sudden cloudburst. They bounced off brollies, hopped on pavements and headed in their hundreds to the nearest rivers. Local gardens were full of them.

One elderly lady was moved to report the fall

of frogs to the Gloucestershire Trust For Nature Conservation. The Trust sent naturalist Ian Darling to investigate. He reported that the frogs were each no more than a few grammes in weight and, despite their odd appearance, harmless.

The frogs, it seemed, were pink rather than the usual green because they were albinos – creatures with no colouring at all in their skin. If this seemed like a contradiction, Mr Darling explained that the pink colour came from the blood that showed through the pale skin.

Stroud's pink frogfall was the second weirdness of this type. Two weeks earlier there had been at least one rain of pink frogs in Cirencester, a town not too far away. Some sources claimed there were two. These frogfalls coincided, more or less, with dustfalls over England carried by high winds from the Sahara.

This led the Gloucestershire Trust for Nature Conservation to speculate that the two might be connected. They claimed desert frogs buried themselves in the sand to escape the heat and were there dyed a reddish pink by crystals.

According to the Stroud *Observer*, the Trust considered it possible that the frogs were carried from the Sahara in atmospheric water droplets, but it is difficult to see how atmospheric water droplets formed over the Sahara, one of the driest areas on the face of the planet. It is also

difficult to see how frogs could have survived a journey that would have lasted twenty hours even if they were moving at a consistent 60 miles per hour.

2. Pink frogfalls are seriously weird, but rains of ordinary frogs happen so often they are almost commonplace.

D. F. Garner, of Baltimore, Maryland, in the USA, was driving through a thunderstorm in Pennsylvania when dozens of tiny frogs pelted his car.

When F. J. McManus was growing up on a farm in Minnesota, a storm blew up that looked serious enough for everybody to take cover in the cellar. When it blew over, the family came out to find the ground covered in tiny frogs and fish.

Back in England, Mrs Vida McWilliam witnessed a frog fall during the summer of 1979 at her home in Bedford. The weather turned foul one Sunday with heavy rain and high winds. The rain had stopped the next morning, but when Mrs McWilliam looked out her patio was covered in frogs. Later she discovered more frogs in her garden. They were tiny, some green, some black in colour. Oddly enough, several bushes were covered in frog spawn.

W. A. Walker of Evansville, Indiana, claimed in a letter to a newspaper that in the summer of 1926 he was caught in a sudden thunderstorm while out on the golf course. Suddenly, along with the rain, the golfers were pelted with thousands of small, live frogs.

Frogs also fell on Leicester, Massachusetts, in 1953.

3. In 1578, large yellow mice plunged from the sky at Bergen in Norway. A year later, the good citizens had to endure a rainfall of lemmings, rodents closely related to voles and meadow mice. Lemmings measure 8–13 cm (3–5 in) in length.

4. Burning sulphur rained down on the terrified inhabitants of Magdeburg, Germany, in 1642, causing fires and widespread panic.

5. In 1665, blue fibres with all the appearance of silk thread fell on Naumburg, Germany.

6. Not quite frogs this time. Back in 1683 there was a rainfall of toads over Norfolk, England. Toads also fell in Lalain, France, in 1794 and in Poitiers, France, in 1809.

7. In 1687, the east coast of the Baltic Sea was the site of one of the most bizarre "snowfalls" ever. Huge dark flakes, most of them as big as table tops, floated down from the sky. Experts later found they were composed of black algae and infusoria, tiny plants that grow in dense patches. Nobody had any idea where they came from.

8. A foul smelling, greasy substance with the appearance of rancid butter fell in Ireland in 1696.

9. In 1786 the capital of Haiti, Port-au-Prince, was pelted with a heavy rain of black eggs.

10. The Scots are noted for their fondness for herring, which may go some way towards explaining the rainfall of herring at Argylshire in 1817. Or may not.

11. In Iran, then known as Persia, there was a fall of animal feed in 1828.

12. Some weird weather can be positively dangerous. Citizens of Marsala in Sicily were forced to take cover in 1835 when subjected to a hail of stones from the sky. Not hailstones, which are made from ice, but real stones made from rock.

13. Shanghai is China's largest city and one of the world's great ports with a population of over 11 million. Rainfall averages about 115cm every year, most of it falling during the monsoon. But in 1846, all of Shanghai and approximately 1,500 square miles of surrounding countryside were covered in a fine drizzle of olive-grey powder.

14. Daft though it sounds, there was a rain of beef on San Francisco in 1851.

15. In 1857, cinders fell on Ottawa, Illinois. This was followed by lizards raining on Sacramento, California in 1870, snakes on

Memphis, Tennessee in 1877 and worms on Randolph County, West Virginia in 1891.

16. Not to be outdone, residents of Hendon, England reported a downpour of sand eels in 1918.

17. Silver coins poured down on Meshchera, Russia, in 1940. Seventeen years later it was raining 1,000-franc banknotes on Bourges, France, while in 1976, Limburg, Germany, also had a rain of banknotes.

18. In 1961 green peaches fell on Shreveport, Louisiana.

19. Mud, wood, glass and pottery all poured down on Pinar del Rio in Cuba during one of the more varied of weird rains in 1968.

• There's a lot more debris in our atmosphere than most people imagine. Algae, insect eggs, hair, feathers and much more are skimmed from the surface of the earth by relatively light winds.

• Scientists will try to convince you weird rains are caused by whirlwinds and waterspouts (great spinning columns of water hundreds of metres high taken up from the sea by high winds). A tornado can reach speeds of 300 mph and generate enormous pressure – more than enough to lift and carry some unlikely things, like the pink frogs.

• There are confirmed reports of a church spire swept a distance of seventeen miles, a chicken coop carried for four and a 272kg wooden beam tossed a quarter of a mile by tornadoes.

• In England, observers saw fish being blown out of a lake on to land during a storm, while in Norway, a harbour was almost emptied of water – and anything living in it – by the action of a waterspout.

• All the same, most bizarre rains aren't mixtures. You'll notice only the Pinar del Rio fall (number 19 in our Fact File) involved more than one thing. Fish fall without seaweed, sand and other litter you'd expect to find if they were scooped up by a waterspout.

• Almost all the fish, frogs and other creatures that rain down remain alive and well. How do they survive a whirlwind? How do the fish survive out of water?

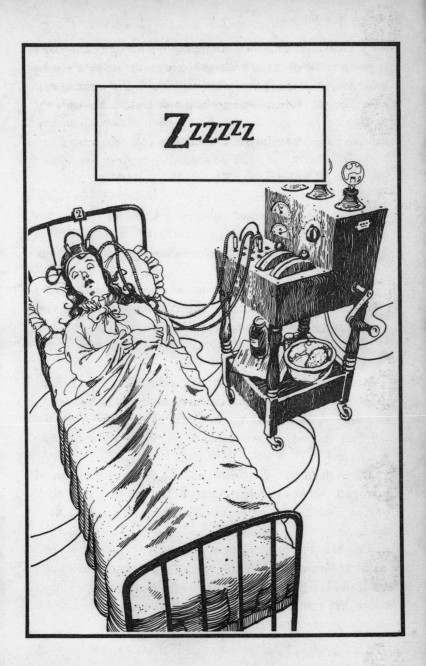

Sleep has always been a bit of a mystery. As a baby, you spend most of your time asleep. As an adult, you sleep on average seven or eight hours a night. In old age you sleep less — maybe four to six hours a night. But nobody really knows why you do it at all. You could rest perfectly well just by putting your feet up. But if all sleep is a mystery, some sleep is positively weird. Take this case. . . .

Sweden, 22 February, 1876

Fourteen-year-old Swedish schoolgirl, Carolina Olsson, was on her way home to the family cottage at Oknö, near Mönsteras, in February, 1876, when she slipped on the ice and fell, hitting her head.

By the time she got home, she had a nasty headache and a couple of days later started to complain about tiredness. Her mother put her to bed.

On the evening of 22 February, 1876, Carolina fell asleep. She slept soundly until 3 April, 1908.

For the first couple of days and nights, Carolina's parents debated about calling the doctor. Her father was a fisherman, far from rich, and wasn't sure he could afford the fee. They fed her milk and sugared water and hoped she would eventually wake up.

When she didn't, they finally called a doctor. He examined her, stuck needles into her fingers to test for a reaction, then pronounced his diagnosis. The girl, he said, was in a deep sleep.

This was the first of many unhelpful medical opinions. Word of Carolina's condition went the rounds and more and more doctors took an interest. Many had their own ideas about her condition. They said she was supposed to be suffering from paralysis or faking.

But no one had any idea how to wake her up.

In desperation, her parents brought her to Oskarshamn Hospital where the doctors tried to wake her by giving her electric shocks. When that didn't work, they sent her home. Her condition, they said, was incurable.

One night her father came in from work to discover Carolina kneeling by the sofa where she slept, praying to Jesus. He was overjoyed until he realized she was not awake, but sleepwalking. When she finished her prayers, she climbed back into bed.

The family kept feeding her milk and sugared water. Carolina kept sleeping. When her mother died in 1908, a widowed neighbour came in to help with the housekeeping.

On 3 April, 1908, thirty-two years and forty-two days after she dozed off, Carolina eventually awoke. The housekeeper found her wandering about the cottage looking for her mother.

It was a painful awakening. Not only was her mother gone, but two of her brothers were also dead, the result of a drowning accident. She could not believe that her father was now old and her remaining brothers middle-aged. She remembered them as they had been more than thirty years before.

Oddly enough, while her family had aged, Carolina hadn't – or at least not at anything like the same rate. Her body still looked like that of a fourteen-year-old and while her face seemed a little older, nobody would have taken her for anything older than her middle twenties, although she was in fact forty-six.

Not surprisingly, Carolina found herself famous. The newspapers dubbed her Sleeping Beauty (she was a very pretty girl) and tourists turned up by the coachload just to catch a glimpse of her.

She was a little weak and dizzy immediately after wakening, but demanded a meal of herring and quickly recovered.

Some two years after her ordeal she was examined by a doctor from Stockholm. He found her intelligent and cheerful, healthy and co-operative. She still looked far younger than her actual age and had a clear memory of her life before she fell asleep.

Her life after she woke up again proved long and happy. She survived a further forty-two years and died, aged 89, in April, 1950.

• One of the oddest aspects of Carolina Olsson's weird experience was that neither her hair, her toe-nails nor her fingernails grew while she was asleep. This is particularly bizarre when you remember that the fingernails and hair of a corpse continue to grow for some time after death.

• Although widely studied, Carolina's condition was a mystery to the medical profession and remains so today. Although she was often referred to as being in a coma, this actually seems unlikely: most coma victims die without regaining consciousness, or are disabled when they do waken. Carolina's sleep gave her no problems at all.

• Unless you follow Carolina's example, you will spend about a third of your life sleeping. This means that if you live as long as she did, you will have rested about thirty years in the Land of Nod. If this sounds surprisingly close to Carolina's own record, you have to remember she stayed asleep for thirty-two years *continuously.* Furthermore, she would *already* have spent approximately four to five of her previous fourteen years in normal sleep. When she woke after her big sleep, her normal sleep pattern would account for a further twelve years until the time of her death. So Carolina Olsson, at 89, actually spent about fifty years sleeping during her lifetime.

1. Although Carolina Olsson holds the world record for the longest sleep, the record for the longest stay in bed goes to an Italian named Bettina Pieri. Bettina was just fifteen years old when she took to her bed and refused point blank to get up again. She stayed there, sleeping for three or four years at a time, and developed miraculous powers – or at least so her neighbours believed. People came to her to be cured – and often were. Bettina's hair turned white. At the age of 88 she died . . . having stayed in bed for 73 years.

2. By contrast, an American named Al Herpin lived into his nineties without ever having slept at all. The tar-paper shack where he lived outside Trenton, New Jersey, USA, had no bedroom and no bed. When he got tired at night, he would sit in his old rocking chair and read until he felt rested, but he never nodded off. Doctors who examined him found him to be in good health with above average intelligence.

3. In 1971, James McDonnell was involved in a car accident and suffered from concussion. It obviously wasn't his year, because a few months later he suffered head injuries from a second accident. Not surprisingly he developed a headache. He told a friend he was going for a walk to try to clear it. When he failed to return after seven years, he was declared dead by the Courts. But *fifteen* years later, on Christmas Day, 1985, his wife answered the doorbell to find James standing on the step. He explained that he had bumped his head the day before and suddenly became conscious of where he was (Philadelphia) and that his first name was James. Gradually the rest of his memory returned. Experts believe this sort of condition, in which you have no idea who you are, shares some characteristics with sleep. In a sense, McDonnell seems to have been sleepwalking for fifteen years.

4. The French eccentric Henri Rochatain spent six months living and sleeping on a tightrope in 1973. The rope was stretched more than twenty-five metres above a car park in Saint Etienne. M. Rochatain furnished it with a chemical loo and a board for a bed, both of which were simply balanced on the rope, not attached to it in any way. During his six months, he managed to sleep through thunderstorms and high winds while astonished doctors monitored his brain waves via electrodes wired to his skull. If he had so much as turned over in his sleep, he would have fallen to his death on the concrete below. But he survived to try out an even more bizarre stunt – walking four thousand miles around France on stilts.

5. Mark Henderson, a 14-year-old Burnley schoolboy, went for a walk one evening. But

Mark was fast asleep at the time and woke to find himself on the *roof* of his home. He had somehow managed to climb out of a tiny window and walk three metres down slippery slates (it was raining at the time) before he was spotted by neighbours on the very edge of the roof. The Fire Brigade brought him down with a ladder.

6. Muggers who attacked Conley Holbrook in North Carolina in 1983 thought they had got away with their crime. They beat him unconscious and left him for dead. But eight years later he woke up and told the police who did it.

7. When Tina Houghton was still a baby in her mother's womb, she went into a unique four-month hibernation during which she stopped growing, but proceeded to develop normally afterwards. She was born a tiny, sleepy baby. She never woke in the night for a feed and even during the day she slept most of the time. Today, as an adult, she sleeps until lunchtime unless she has to go to work and takes a nap in the afternoon when she comes home.

Dream of Death

If sleep is a mystery, dreaming is probably the most peculiar occupation of all. When you dream, you pass into an odd state in which you firmly believe yourself to be somewhere else, often doing things you'd never dream of doing in waking life. But the weird thing is that some dreams seem to be connected with your waking life in a wholly impossible way. Like this dream, which visited two people in Victorian England. . .

London, England, 11 May, 1812

Britain's Prime Minister, Spencer Perceval, was walking through the lobby of the House of Commons on the morning of 11 May, 1812, when he became the victim of a successful assassination attack.

A man stepped from behind a pillar brandishing a gun and, before anyone could intervene, shot the Prime Minister dead.

The act stunned the nation. Unlike many other heads of state, British prime ministers were not then thought of as prime targets for assassination.

It came as no surprise to learn that the assassin himself was insane. He had for some time been nursing an imaginary grievance against the government that Spencer Perceval headed.

The history books record that Perceval was succeeded by his then secretary of war, Robert Banks Jenkinson, the second Earl of Liverpool, who became one of the longest-serving prime ministers the country ever had.

What is not (usually) recorded is the weirdness associated with Spencer Perceval's sudden, violent death.

On May 3, 1812, a wealthy gentleman named John Williams was enjoying life on his extensive estate at Redruth, in Cornwall. He was a man with little or no interest in politics, his days being occupied with the management of his estate and the hunting-shooting pursuits of a country squire.

But on the night of 3 May, Williams dreamed a strange dream. In it, Williams was standing in a cloakroom of the House of Commons when he witnessed a violent, unexpected scene.

Before he could do anything about it, a small, bushy-haired man in a dark green coat with bright brass buttons pulled a pistol from his pocket and shot a passerby in the chest.

The victim fell to the floor and Williams watched in horror as he died.

In his dream, the horrified Williams gripped a bystander and demanded to know the name of the man who had been killed. It was, he was told solemnly, the Prime Minister of Great Britain, Spencer Perceval.

Williams woke up with a start. His wife in the bed beside him immediately asked what was wrong. A shaking Williams told her the details of his dream.

Mrs Williams calmed and reassured him. It was, she said, only a dream, probably brought on by something he had eaten at supper. Williams eventually relaxed and drifted back to sleep.

To his horror he found himself in the cloakroom of the House of Commons. A small man in a dark green coat drew a pistol and, before Williams could move to stop him, shot the Prime Minister, Spencer Perceval.

A sweating Williams jerked upright in the bed again, but this time he took care not to waken his wife. For a long time he lay staring at the ceiling and trying to make sense of his nightmare.

He did not know the Prime Minister personally. He had not been thinking of him before he fell asleep. Why should he dream about him not once, but twice? And why should he dream something almost unthinkable – that the Prime Minister was killed?

With these questions still churning in his mind, John Williams slid into a fitful sleep just before morning . . . and dreamed he was standing in a cloakroom in the House of Commons.

For a third time, the terrifying events unfolded before his dreaming eyes. For a third time he was utterly unable to do anything to stop the Prime Minister's assassination.

Next morning, Williams was so disturbed by the triple nightmare that he talked it over with friends. Although not a superstitious man, he began to wonder if it might not be a portent, an omen, a warning. He was well aware of the story of Julius Caesar whose assassination on the Ides of March had been predicted by a soothsayer.

Cas. Who is it in the press that calls on me?
I hear a tongue, shriller than all the music,
Cry, Cæsar!—Speak: Cæsar is turn'd to hear.
Sooth. Beware the ides of March.
Cas.   What man is that?
Bru. A soothsayer, bids you beware the ides of
      March.
Cas. Set him before me; let me see his face.   20
Cas. Fellow, come from the throng: look upon
      Cæsar.
Cas. What say'st thou to me now? Speak once
      again.
Sooth. Beware the ides of March.
Cas. He is a dreamer; let us leave him:—pass.
      [*Sennet. Exeunt all but* BRUTUS *and* CASSIUS.
Cas. Will you go see the order of the course?

He considered driving to London to warn the Prime Minister. His friends persuaded him against it. In the days before the motor car, a trip from Cornwall to London was a costly, difficult event.

Williams then asked if he should write Spencer Perceval a letter explaining about the dreams and asking him to be careful. His friends talked him out of this course of action too. He would, they said, make himself a laughing stock.

Reluctantly, Williams agreed to forget the whole thing. The Prime Minister received no warning . . . at least, not from Cornwall.

But on the night of 10–11 May, Spencer Perceval himself had a dream. In it, he was walking through the lobby of the House of Commons when he was suddenly confronted by a small, bushy-haired man in a dark green coat with brightly-polished brass buttons.

The intruder pulled a pistol from his pocket, pointed it at the Prime Minister and fired. As the bullets struck, everything went black. In his dream, Spencer Perceval concluded he had been killed.

When he woke on the morning of 11 May, Perceval told his family about the dream. They were a great deal more worried about it than he was and begged him not to attend the sitting of Parliament that day.

Perceval dismissed their fears. The work of the House was important. His presence was needed. There could be no question of staying away simply because of a ridiculous dream.

And so, later that morning, Britain's Prime Minister walked through the lobby of the House of Commons and met death at the hands of an assassin.

Who turned out to be a small, bushy-haired man wearing a dark green coat with shiny brass buttons.

1. In April 1986, a British Court acquitted a man charged with the murder of his 33-year-old wife . . . on the grounds that he had done the deed while dreaming. In his dream he was being chased through a jungle by two soldiers who were trying to kill him. They caught up with him and there was a violent struggle. In the dream one of the soldiers was armed with a knife, the other with a gun. The sleeper grappled with them and tried to strangle the soldier who had the knife. Then the gunman fired and he woke up, only to find he had throttled his wife.

2. Your eyes move rapidly from side to side when you dream, leading scientists to refer to dreaming as REM (Rapid Eye Movement) sleep. Research has shown this movement relates to whatever you happen to be looking at in the dream.

3. One of the most famous poems of Samuel Taylor Coleridge, the epic *Kubla Khan*, was composed during a dream. The poet woke and was in the process of getting it down on paper when he was disturbed by a visitor. By the time the man left, the rest of the dream had been forgotten, leaving the work forever unfinished. The novelist Robert Louis Stevenson had better luck. He dreamed – and remembered – the plot of the work that made him famous, *Dr Jeckyll and Mr Hyde*.

4. Everybody dreams every night. The reason many people don't believe this is that dreams are very quickly forgotten so that it often *seems* we have spent a night without dreaming.

5. It takes about 90 minutes after you fall asleep for you to experience your first dream, and there is more than an hour's delay between your first dream of the night and your second. But this period grows shorter and shorter as the night wears on so that you do most of your dreaming just before you wake up in the morning.

6. Science and technology have both benefited greatly from dreams. The chemist Friedrich August Kekule von Stradonitz finally figured out what a benzene molecule looked like after dreaming of a snake swallowing its tail. The inventor of the sewing machine got his idea of putting the eye of the needle at the point when he dreamed he was being boiled and eaten by cannibals. As the cannibals danced around the pot, he noticed the points of their spears all had needle eyes. Swiss-born Louis Agassiz, the naturalist who discovered the world had been gripped by various Ice Ages in the distant past, accurately dreamed the appearance of an obscure prehistoric fish. The dream was so vivid he was able to draw the fish when he awoke . . . and he then used his drawing as a guide to cracking open a stone which revealed a perfect fossil of the fish.

7. When BBC cameraman Graham Tidman visited Hole House, near Branscombe, England, in May 1964, to do a documentary on water divining, he was astonished to discover he knew the place well, even though he had never been there before and had no friends or relatives in the area. Tidman had, in fact, dreamed about the house on no fewer than five occasions prior to visiting it in reality. But in his dreams he never saw the place as it was in 1964, but rather as it *had been* when it was built in 1896 . . . many years before he was born. Architect's plans confirmed Tidman's dreams had been absolutely accurate.

8. A retired English engineer, J. W. Dunne, became famous in the 1930s for his book *An Experiment With Time,* in which he outlined many case studies of his own and other people's dreams of events in the future. These included disasters like ships sinking and volcanic eruptions. The weird thing was that Dunne did not dream about the events themselves but about the newspaper reports on them. His dreams did take place before the events and the news reports about them, but the dreams were not eye-witness accounts: they were based on the information in the newspapers. Eventually Dunne concluded that dreams can be made up of elements from the dreamer's past, present and *future,* but distorted so that they are often not recognized as such.

9. While still a student at Balliol College, Oxford, John Godley (who later became Lord Kilbracken) developed the useful knack of dreaming winners at horse races. The first time it happened – on 8 March, 1946 – he dreamed of two horses, bet on the first and, when it won, transferred his winnings on to the second . . . which also won. The dream netted him more than £100, a small fortune in those days. Although he could not do it to order, Godley continued to dream of winners from time to time right up to 1958 when, after his largest-ever win, the talent left him.

10. During the 1950s, Mr and Mrs Butler went house-hunting in Ireland following a series of dreams in which Mrs Butler "saw" the house where she wanted to live. Eventually they found it in reality. Mrs Butler told the estate agent to be quiet while she described the interior of the house perfectly. She made only one "mistake". She said there was a green door in a room where no door existed . . . but the estate agent confirmed there *had* been a door there which had recently been bricked up. The house was large and the Butlers were far from sure they could afford it, but when they asked the price the agent quoted a ridiculously small sum. They asked why it was going so cheaply and the man finally admitted that the house was haunted. Then he added, "But don't worry, Mrs Butler – *you're* the ghost!" It appeared that while she had been dreaming of the house, her ghostly form had been seen walking through it.

11. The distinguished Victorian scholar, Sir E. A. Wallis Budge, got an early boost to his career as the result of a dream. As a young student, too poor to pay his own way, he entered a competition which had a university scholarship as its prize. The night before he was to sit the examination, he dreamed three times of the questions he would be asked next day, including the ancient texts he would be asked to translate. These texts were peculiar in that they were printed on green paper. Budge woke up at two in the morning and began to study the texts he had dreamed about. Sure enough, the next day, the examination did indeed involve the same texts and questions . . . but more than that, the examination hall was exactly as he had dreamed and the texts were even printed on green paper.

12. In 1863, an American manufacturer named Wilmot was on board the *City of Limerick* when the ship hit a mid-Atlantic storm. During the night, he dreamed his wife visited him in her nightdress and kissed him.

Although he had said nothing of the dream, his cabin mate teased him the following morning about his midnight visit from a lady. When he arrived home in Bridgeport Connecticut, his wife at once asked him if he had received a visit from her in the night. She had, she said, been worried by reports of shipwrecks and decided to try to find out if he was safe.

She visualized herself flying over the ocean, finding the ship and going to his cabin. A man in the upper berth looked straight at her, but she

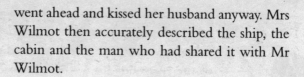

went ahead and kissed her husband anyway. Mrs Wilmot then accurately described the ship, the cabin and the man who had shared it with Mr Wilmot.

The Chinese Dragon

In the old days, before the world was fully explored, map-makers used to fill up the places they knew nothing about with legends like "Here Be Dragons". Everybody believed in dragons in those days, so the claim was a sort of Keep Out notice. Most of the time, of course, there were no dragons. But sometimes. . .

Hubei Province, China, May, 1995

During May and June of 1995, the Chinese Academy of Sciences sent a full-scale expedition into the remote mountain region of Hubei Province . . . to search for a dragon.

Up to then, even Chinese scientists had dismissed dragons as imaginary, but the Hubei dragon, called a *shui guai* (water dragon), was seen so often that the authorities were forced to take the reports seriously.

It was first mentioned in documents dating back to the third century but no one in modern times paid very much attention.

Then, in 1962, fishermen tossed explosives into the fast-flowing river at the bottom of a gorge in the Hubei mountains. They were trying to stun fish so they would be easy to net, but disturbed something very different.

To their horror and astonishment, a hideous creature rose up out of the water. It was no fish, it wasn't stunned and it was far from amused.

According to eye-witness reports, the thing was about as ugly as it was possible to get. It had a flat head and its protruding eyes were as big as lanterns. There was a patch of red hair or fur across its shoulders.

One of the fishermen called out "*Chan! Chan!*" a word that means "toad". And the thing did indeed look a bit like an exceptionally ugly, giant toad. It shook the water off its back and began to lumber towards the men.

The fishermen held their ground for all of thirty seconds, then fled. But infuriated by the explosives, the great chan came after them.

It chased them all the way into the Shennongjia National Forest where, eventually, they escaped.

But that was not the end of it. Now it had been disturbed, the creature seemed to have no intention of returning to its underwater haunts. Workers and others with business in the National Forest began to send back increasingly frequent reports of having seen – and sometimes having been chased by – something very weird.

Although local fishermen clung to the nickname chan, it soon became obvious the brute was no toad, giant or otherwise.

As sighting followed sighting, a description built up of a creature with webbed hands, more or less the shape of a human's, although far fatter.

An idea of its size can be drawn from the fact that its feet – webbed, with lengthy nails or claws – were said to be as big as bathtubs.

But the authorities began to suspect they might be dealing with a dragon when witnesses spoke of a mouth more than a metre wide from which it exhaled long plumes of white vapour.

Dragons appear in many old myths and legends. Typically they are thought to have scaly bodies like reptiles, but descriptions vary. They usually breathe smoke and flame and are associated with water.

Scientists analysing the reports concluded that the white vapour breathed out by this creature from the water might easily be mistaken for smoke and started to wonder if close encounters with animals of this type were the basis of all the old dragon legends.

Eventually they decided to send an expedition to find out. Professor Lui Minzhuang of the Shanghai East China University stated that he believed the monster to be a survivor from Stone Age times when the Hubei region lay under water.

Meanwhile, local residents continue to think twice before venturing too near the dragon's lair.

• Stories of dragons are surprisingly widespread. They form part of the mythology of Europe and China, and dragons appear as the flying serpent of the Australian Aborigines and of pre-Columbian South America, as the North American Indians' Thunderbird and ancient Egypt's Apep. The earliest examples of dragons are found in the religious epics of two of our most ancient cultures – the Hindu *Rig Veda* and the Babylonian legend of the Marduk.

• Most dragons are thought of as evil, but in China some are held to be good so that the dragon became the symbol of the Emperor.

• In ancient China, *lung mei* or "dragon lines" were invisible tracks believed to carry currents of good luck. Only the Emperor was allowed to be buried on a dragon line. Commoners buried on one were dug up again and their families executed.

• The Komodo dragon, which is the world's largest lizard, can grow up to three metres in length and normally weighs around 136 kilograms. These dragons are natives of Indonesia and feed on animals as large as deer and pigs. They were long thought harmless to humans, but recently it was discovered they have attacked local people and even eaten the occasional tourist.

• Dinosaurs, which were the dominant life form on our planet for 140 million years, became extinct 65 million years ago, possibly as the result of a comet colliding with the Earth. But there are persistent rumours that a few survived and bred. The famous naturalist Sir Peter Scott went on record with his belief that the Loch Ness Monster was a plesiosaur.

1. In 1898 zoologist Dr Peter Olsson noted several newspaper articles about a strange creature in the Jamtlands province of Sweden. Over the next few years he accumulated twenty-two accounts which he felt came from trustworthy witnesses. Eye-witness accounts of the creature have continued up to the present with the latest rash of sightings in 1965. The creature is said to have a two- to two-and-a-half-metre-long neck attached to a four-metre-long body. It is grey in colour, appears to be furred and has a horse-like head. It seems to have its home in Lake Storsjo.

2. The Shushwap tribe of British Columbia have an age-old tradition of a beast called the Naitaka which lives in Lake Okanagan. There are three ancient carvings on stones around the lake depicting the monster. The stories sound like one more of those old familiar Indian myths except for one thing – there have been nearly two hundred sightings of the creature since Europeans arrived in the 1700s. In 1934, Captain House of the Canadian Fishery Patrol described it as looking like a telegraph pole with a sheep's head. Vancouver resident Mrs Campbell saw it in 1952 but thought its head was more like that of a cow or a horse. In 1967, the Durrant family from White Rock, British Columbia watched it through binoculars and reported that it appeared to be chasing a school of fish.

3. On 13 January, 1852, Captain Seabury of the whaler *Monongahela* sent three longboats to investigate what he believed to be a surfaced whale. He harpooned the animal before he discovered his mistake. An enormous head rose from the water and lunged at the boats. Two were capsized. The monster was unlike anything the crew had ever seen. Its body was estimated to be thirty-six metres long – longer than the *Monongahela* itself – and eighteen metres around. The three-metre-thick neck supported a reptilian head containing a large number of eight-centimetre teeth. The body was brownish grey with a metre-wide light stripe running its length. It had no fins or legs but there was a knobbly, four-and-a-half-metre tail.

4. The commercial fishing ship Zuiyo Maru was off New Zealand's coast in April 1977, when it caught a large, unknown creature that had apparently died in the nets. The crew hoisted the carcass from the water and took colour pictures before the Captain ordered the bizarre beast to be dropped back into the sea for fear of contaminating his cargo. Professor Tokio Shikmama of Yokahama National University examined the photographs and declared the corpse was neither fish nor any known mammal.

5. A hundred years ago, the headman of the Caucasian village of Tkhinaa was presented with a "wild girl" captured by a hunter. Named Zana by her captors, the girl grew large and powerful and eventually learned to carry firewood, water and sacks of grain. She was very tall, completely covered with hair, and never managed to speak. Zana died in the 1880s and was buried outside the village. In 1964 Professor Boris Porshenev and a team of Soviet scientists excavated her grave. Their report states the skeleton was of a female creature which was not human.

Large, fur-covered humanoid creatures known as Sasquatch or Bigfoot in North America, or Yeti in the Himalayas, are believed by some scientists to be survivors of Neanderthal humanity, a widespread sub-species of prehistoric humans that inhabited Europe and parts of Asia and North Africa from about 125,000 to about 40,000 years ago. Most scientists, however, dismiss them as myths.

6. Wounded and captured by Chinese hunters in 1913, a creature was held in a cage at Patang in Sinkiang province for several months. It was described as having a black face, 10cm long silvery yellow hair and exceptionally large, powerful hands and feet which were much closer to human hands than those of an ape. After five months it sickened and died.

7. During the early 1940s, Pennsylvania author Robert Lyman saw an odd creature sitting in a road. It looked like a very large vulture, brown, with a short neck and very narrow wings. After a while it spread wings measuring twenty feet and rose into the air, then flew into the woods. In 1969, Mrs John Boyle was sitting on her remote cabin porch enjoying the view near Little Pine Creek when a huge, grey coloured bird landed in the creek. She said the bird's wingspan was nearly as wide as the creek . . . which would have made it fully 25 metres. After a while the bird rose and flew back into the woods.

Many North American Indian tribes take giant flying creatures for granted. They call them "Thunderbirds" because the noise made by their enormous wings sounds like thunder.

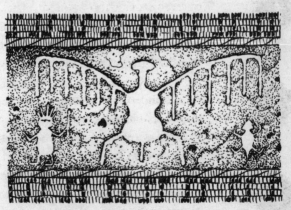

8. At 2 a.m. on 17 January, 1909, John McOwen of Bristol, Pennsylvania, USA, looked from his bedroom window and saw ". . . a large creature standing on the banks of the canal. It looked something like an eagle and hopped along the path." A little later a Bristol police officer, James Sackville, also saw something he described as ". . . winged, hopping like a bird, but which had strange features and a horrible scream." That same morning, the postmaster witnessed the creature flying across the Delaware River and reported, "Its head resembled that of a ram, with curled horns, and its long thick neck was thrust forward in flight. It had long, thin wings and short legs, the front legs shorter than the hind. Again, it uttered its mournful and awful call – a combination of a squawk and a whistle." The next morning numerous Bristol residents found the creature's hoof-like footprints in the snow.

9. During the First World War, Mr and Mrs Scarberry were driving at night with friends in West Virginia, USA, when they saw two circles reflecting red in the headlights. As they got closer, they were astounded to see the circles were eyes belonging to a man–shaped creature. It walked upright on two legs and shuffled towards them. They estimated it to be two metres or more in height, grey in colour and possessing enormous drooping wings. The creature seen by the Scarberrys has turned up in many areas of the United States. In most reports it is referred to as "The Mothman".

10. The first sightings of a weird flying creature in Texas were made on New Year's Day, 1976, but were not taken seriously. The witnesses were Harlingen residents Jackie Davis and Tracey Lawson, fourteen and eleven years old respectively. They claimed to have seen a giant bird 1.5 metres high, with shoulders wider than a man's. It was dark coloured, had a bald head with big red eyes and a gorilla-like face. Their parents accompanied them the next day to check the area where the "bird" had been seen. To their amazement they found three-toed tracks nearly eight inches across pressed deeply into the ground.

11. James Powell, an explorer and crocodile expert, is convinced dragons may be representatives of long-extinct dinosaurs. He came to this conclusion after investigating rumours of a dinosaur-like creature seen by members of remote tribes in the jungles of Africa.

On a trip to the former French West African colony of Gabon, he travelled up the Ogooue river and visited an elderly native witch doctor. Powell showed him a picture of a diplodocus, one of the best known of all the dinosaurs.

The man told him it was well-known in the region where the natives called it a "N'yamala". Hardly able to believe what he was hearing, Powell tried the same picture on natives from different tribes in the area. All of them recognized the creature.

He was told his dinosaur was very secretive, that it lived in the most remote marshes and rivers, and fed mostly on "jungle chocolate", a plant that grows near water and bears large nut-like fruits.

12. The *N'yamala's* description sounds exactly like that of another African mystery animal, the *Mokele-mbembe*. Natives of the Cameroons talk about an enormous four-legged creature that sounds to Western scientists suspiciously like a brontosaurus.

Captain Freiherr von Stein zu Lausnitz collected the earliest reports in 1913. They described an animal larger than an elephant with smooth skin and a long, flexible neck and tail. It grew to about ten metres long and lived in underwater caves along the river.

One expedition was told by a local tribe that a few years ago a dead *Mokele-mbembe* was found in the river. The tribesmen cut it up and ate it, but became ill as a result and a few died. They threw the remains into the river to appease the animal's ghost and help cure the sick.

Though neither *Mokele-mbembe* nor *N'yamala* have been photographed, their tracks have been found.

13. In February, 1993, the *Florida Sun* reported that a Russian Air Force General claimed three Russian cosmonauts were sent to the moon on a secret mission to expose a cover-up by the

American Space Administration NASA.

They brought back evidence that members of the first Apollo mission had found the remains of a giant dinosaur half buried in the moon dust.

Very few people believe the story.

A Hitch in Time

Time travel seems to be a popular movie theme these days. Usually the hero manages it with the help of some amazing high-tech machinery that hums and flashes coloured lights. But in this weird real world, time travel doesn't happen like that at all. As you'll discover in our next case study.

France, August, 1901

On a hot August afternoon in 1901, two respectable Victorian ladies, on holiday in France set out to explore the Palace of Marie Antoinette in Versailles.

The ladies were Miss Charlotte Anne Elizabeth Moberly, Principal of St Hugh's Hall at the University of Oxford and Miss Eleanor Frances Jourdain, a teacher with her own girl's school in Watford. Miss Jourdain had a rented flat in Paris.

On 10 August, the two companions boarded a train for Versailles.

They spent much of the day touring the palace itself, then rested in the Salle des Glaces. It was not until about four in the afternoon that Miss Moberly suggested they should visit the Petit Trianon one of the smaller palaces at Versailles.

The Petit Trianon, lies about a kilometre and a half north-west of the main palace. The two ladies consulted their guide map and set off to find it.

They arrived eventually at the Grand Trianon, a companion building. Instead of turning right as they should have done, they then went straight ahead and entered a narrow lane running roughly at right angles to the main drive.

After walking around the outside of a number of buildings, they asked directions from two men they thought were gardeners.

They were told to go straight on, but somehow made a detour to the left. They passed a smallish building they described as a "kiosk" (but which they later decided must have been the Temple de l'Amour) and there, quite suddenly, began to feel distinctly weird.

For Miss Moberly the feeling was one of sadness which she could not understand. Not wanting to spoil the outing, she said nothing about it, but Miss Jourdain was just as uncomfortable. She found the place lonely and depressing. She felt as if she was sleepwalking.

They continued on and met a number of people who seemed to be wearing very old-fashioned clothing. When they asked directions (in French) both noticed these people pronounced the words oddly. Miss Jourdain thought one man used an old form of the language.

They came out eventually into the front drive and the odd feeling suddenly lifted. Without discussing their experience, they took a carriage to the Hotel des Réservoirs where they had tea.

For a week, neither of them spoke about the Petit Trianon. Then Miss Moberly started to write a letter home and found herself sinking into the same weird mood. On impulse she asked Miss Jourdain if she thought the Petit Trianon was haunted. Miss Jourdain said she did.

At this stage, the two ladies began to compare notes. Then they started to wonder about the way the people had been dressed. Miss Moberly found one woman she'd seen was not seen at all by Miss Jourdain even though they'd walked right up to her.

Three years later they returned to Versailles and again visited the Petit Trianon.

On this visit they found it completely changed. But by consulting the guide books and talking to officials, they soon discovered the changes had not been made in the last three years. There should have been no changes at all from their first visit.

The two ladies began to study history books which showed the Trianon as it was in the time of Louis XVI.

At this point they discovered something astonishing. Their first visit, in 1901, had taken them to the Petit Trianon exactly as it had been towards the end of the eighteenth century.

They concluded that one woman they had seen might have been Marie Antoinette herself. But not as a ghost. The only real explanation for their experience was that they had somehow stepped back in time.

• The account of the time slip at Versailles was later published under the title of *An Adventure*. It became a controversial best-seller in the early years of the twentieth century.

• Critics discovered a fancy dress party had been held in the Trianon by a woman named Madame de Greffuhle and claimed Miss Jourdain and Miss Moberly had stumbled into the celebrations.

• The publishers of their book also decided the fancy dress party explained completely what had happened and let their book go out of print.

• Recent investigation has shown the fancy dress party was held seven years before the Trianon visit.

1. The biologist Ivan Sanderson, his wife and their assistant Fred Allsop, were working in Haiti when their car broke down and they were forced to walk home. Sanderson was walking with his wife when, to his astonishment, he saw a number of Elizabethan period three-storied houses of varying types along both sides of the road. It was night, but he saw them quite clearly in bright moonlight. Sanderson's wife saw them too and stopped so abruptly that he walked into her. They noticed that the track on which they were walking had turned suddenly into a properly paved road. Then they began to feel faint. At that point Sanderson called to Fred, who had been walking on ahead. The Sandersons felt dizzy and collapsed on to a tall, rough kerbstone. Fred ran back and doled out cigarettes, by which time the strange houses and the paved road had vanished. Fred, it transpired, had seen nothing unusual.

2. P. J. Chase of Wallington in Surrey was waiting for a bus one afternoon in 1968 and decided to stroll a little way down the road to pass the time. He came across two lovely little thatched cottages with hollyhocks in their gardens. One of them was dated 1837. Next day Chase mentioned the cottages to a friend – only to be told they did not exist. He went to check and found the friend was right. The only buildings at the spot were two brick houses. But when he made enquiries in the area an elderly resident confirmed that the cottages *had* existed. They had been pulled down to make room for the houses years previously.

3. The author Stephen Jenkins tells of an incident near Mounts Bay in Cornwall during which he saw a horde of armed men in ancient clothing skulking in the bushes near the track where he was walking. He ran towards them, felt a sensation like passing through a curtain of warm air, then found the men had gone.

4. In 1912, at the age of 23, the historian Arnold Toynbee was on the summit of Pharsalus Mountain in Greece staring out over the sunlit landscape. Suddenly he found himself back in 197 BC when the forces of Philip of Macedon fought the Roman legions at this spot. For a moment he watched the violent slaughter then the scene disappeared and he was back in a peaceful, sunlit present. Two months later it happened again, this time on Crete. There he travelled 250 years back in time to the day a villa (now long in ruins) had been evacuated and abandoned. A time slip happened to him again at Ephesus while he was inspecting the ruins of an open-air theatre. A month later, on 23 April, he climbed up to the citadel of Monemvasia in Laconia and dropped back in time to 1715 when the citadel had fallen to the Turks. The following month, he was at the ruins of Mistrà in Sparta watching the highland hordes from Màni lay waste to the citadel in the year 1821. These weird experiences led Toynbee to write his 12-volume *Study of History*, which became a classic in its field.

5. In the early winter of 1973, Mrs Jane O'Neill, a Cambridge schoolteacher, visited Fotheringhay Church in Northamptonshire, the place where Mary Queen of Scots was executed. She spent a good deal of time admiring a picture of the Crucifixion behind the altar. It had a peculiar type of arched top.

Some hours later she was in her hotel with a friend named Shirley, who was reading aloud from an essay which referred to the same type of arch. But when Mrs O'Neill mentioned this, her friend, who had visited the church often, told her she had never seen either the arch or the picture. A year later, Jane O'Neill went back to Fotheringhay Church. The outside was exactly as she remembered it, but when she went inside she knew at once she was in a different building. It was much smaller than the church she had visited before. There was no painting of the Crucifixion. Mrs O'Neill got in

touch with a Northamptonshire historian, who told her that the original Fotheringhay Church had been pulled down in 1553 and the present building erected on the site. Further research soon confirmed that the church Mrs O'Neill had entered in 1973 was the one that had been demolished more than four hundred years earlier.

6. The author Joan Forman was in the courtyard of Haddon Hall in Derbyshire in 1974 when she noticed a group of children playing near the door. One of them was a nine-year-old girl in a lace cap and green silk dress. The group disappeared abruptly as she stepped towards them, but when she entered the Hall she discovered a portrait of the girl, the long-dead Lady Grace Manners.

7. In 1954, an English couple, Mr and Mrs Allan, visited an historical church in the village of Wotton Hatch. As they came out of the churchyard, they decided to explore an overgrown path which led uphill to a wooden seat with an excellent view over the valley. They were sitting on this seat eating their sandwiches when Mrs Allan became convinced three men had entered the clearing behind them, one wearing clerical garb. When she tried to turn round to see, she found she was paralysed. After a few moments the feeling passed and the Allans left. In 1956, Mrs Allan went back. She visited the church, but could not find the path to the clearing. The hill she and her husband had climbed was no longer there. Her husband made enquiries and found there was no wooden seat anywhere in the church grounds. The case was officially investigated some years later. Nowhere in the area bore any resemblance to the hill, clearing or bench the Allans described, but there was a 17th century record of three criminals, one a priest, who had been executed there.

8. In 1935, while still a wing commander, Air Marshal Sir Victor Goddard was sent to inspect a disused airfield at Drem, near Edinburgh. He found it in a very dilapidated state with cattle grazing on grass that had forced through cracks in the tarmac. Later that day, he ran into trouble while flying his biplane in heavy rain and decided to return to Drem to get his bearings. As he approached the airfield the torrential rain suddenly changed to bright sunlight. When he looked down he saw the airfield had been completely renovated and was now in use. There were mechanics in blue overalls walking around and four yellow planes parked on the runway. One of these was a model which he did not recognize. Four years later Goddard solved the mystery. With World War Two now raging, he visited Drem again and found it exactly as he had seen it in 1935, complete with blue-overalled mechanics and yellow planes. He even found the plane he had been unable to identify earlier – a Miles Magister.

9. If your twin brother leaves the planet to take a round trip in a spaceship at or near the speed of light, he will be younger than you are when he gets back. This is because time slows down the faster you travel.

10. Plans for a working time machine were published by a respected scientist, Dr Frank Tipler, in 1974. The machine, which is too big to be built anywhere on Earth, consists of a huge cylinder of very dense material. When set spinning, the Tipler Cylinder creates areas which act as gateways to the past and future. The best shape for a timeship which could use the gateways created by a Tipler Cylinder is disc-like. In other words, quite similar to a flying saucer.

Impossible Antique

Archaeology, according to my encyclopaedia, is "an immense and wide-ranging subject that covers a time span of three million years, from the first appearance of humankind to the present day". Three million years is a heck of a long time, but all the same, I sometimes wonder if the archaeologists shouldn't be looking even further back...

Nevada, USA, 1922

During the summer of 1922, John T. Reid, a mining engineer, was out in the wilds of Nevada looking for fossils, the stony remains of prehistoric animals and plants.

While crossing a rocky outcrop, his eye fell on something that caused him to stop in amazement. He knelt down and looked closer.

With mounting excitement he realized he was examining a genuine fossil. It formed part of the actual rock structure and had obviously been there since prehistoric times.

The specimen was not complete. The front part seemed to be missing. But at least two thirds of the overall shape was still there.

Reid stood up and bit his lip. He still could scarcely believe what he was seeing. He had been collecting fossils for years, but this was like nothing he had ever come across before.

He unslung the bag around his shoulder and took out the tools he used in his fossil gathering. Working slowly and nervously, he patiently chipped the astonishing fossil out from the surrounding rock.

When it finally came free he lifted it up with trembling hands. He still could not quite believe what he was looking at.

For this was no fossil of any prehistoric animal or plant. It was the fossil of a human footprint.

And not only a human footprint, but the print of someone who had been wearing shoes.

What Reid was looking at was the remains of a shoe sole so old it had turned to stone.

Now he had the fossil free, he could actually see the stitching that ran around the sole.

There was another line of stitching further on and, towards the back, clear signs of wear on the heel. Reid was in no doubt at all that he had found the remains of an ancient shoe, one that had been well-worn at some time in the distant past.

But while he was certain about the nature of his find, he still could not understand it. People had only worn shoes since the advent of civilization some seven thousand years earlier – far too short a time for anything to fossilize.

What made matters even worse was that Reid knew humanity, with or without shoes, had only been around for about 100,000 years. The rock where he had found his amazing fossil was more than five million years old.

According to the very best scientific theory, only the most distant ancestors of humanity (called hominids) walked the earth five million years ago. These creatures were far closer to apes than to modern people and if anything could be certain about them it was that they did not wear stitched leather shoes.

Reid brought his astonishing find to New York where he showed it to several professors and scientists who specialized in fossil material. All of them agreed the stone of which the fossil was made dated back to the Triassic Period.

Reid then took his fossil to a number of shoe manufacturers for their opinion. They told him he had definitely found the remains of a hand-made shoe sole, possibly leather like today's shoes.

Despite this, Reid could not get his scientific colleagues to take the find seriously. They just could not believe the evidence before their eyes. Since nobody had worn shoes five million years ago, then what Reid had found simply could not be the remains of a shoe.

But Reid was persistent. He arranged to have his fossil analysed and photographed. (The experts he called in did the work privately so their reputation would not suffer.)

The chemical analysis confirmed that the fossil was actually Triassic and not some later piece of stone that had somehow found its way into Triassic rock.

The photographs went even further. They showed detail of the thread and stitching which proved beyond all doubt that this piece of stone had once been part of a shoe.

• Human beings are classified as mammals. According to scientists there were virtually no mammals on earth at the time of the dinosaurs. It was only after the dinosaurs suddenly died out, some 65 million years ago, that a little tree creature about the size of a shrew, managed to start the mammal kingdom. So the idea of a human in the age of the dinosaurs is preposterous.

• There are two kinds of fossil. One is formed when parts of a dead animal – usually bones – gradually turn to stone over millions of years. Under certain conditions, parts of plants can be preserved in the same way. The other type of fossil is known as a trace fossil. These come about when something leaves its mark in the form of a burrow, track, print or trail in material that eventually becomes stone. At first, Reid's find looked very much like a trace fossil – a footprint in mud that turned to rock. But under examination, it became clear that what he had discovered was an actual fossilized part of a shoe.

• In 1922, the Triassic Period was thought to date back about five million years. Today it is dated between 213 and 248 million years ago, making Reid's fossil almost unimaginably older than he believed at the time.

• On 8 October, 1922, Dr W. H. Ballou published an article in the *New York Sunday American* in which he described Reid's find as one of the foremost scientific mysteries of the day. Most other scientists, however, ignored it.

• Sometimes there are so many fossils in one place that we never think of them as fossils at all. For example both the White Cliffs of Dover and the Niobrara Chalk of Kansas are entirely composed of billions of tiny algae fossils. Each one is so small that you could pack millions of them into a single cubic millimetre.

Million Years Ago

550	500	450	400	350	300	250	200	150	100	50

PRECAMBRIAN	CAMBRIAN	ORDOVICIAN	SILURIAN	DEVONIAN	CARBONIFEROUS	PERMIAN	TRIASSIC	JURASSIC	CRETACEOUS	TERTIARY	QUATERNARY

PALEOZOIC			MESOZOIC		CENOZOIC

1. Something that looks exactly like a cricket ball has been found in a mine in the Western Transvaal, South Africa. It is one of several hundred metal balls discovered in this mine. The balls are of two types – one solid blue metal, the other hollow with a white spongy centre. They all look man-made, but are in fact at least 2,800,000,000 years old.

2. Maximilien Melleville, Vice President of the Société Académique of Laon, France, reported in *The Geologist* the discovery of a perfectly formed Early Eocene chalk ball. Both the ball and its immediate surroundings showed signs of having been shaped from a larger block, then freed by a sharp blow – in other words, the ball seems to have been manufactured. Yet its age must be between 45 and 55 million years, again well before the appearance of humanity on the planet.

3. In 1928, a miner named Atlas Almon Mathis was working in a mine near Heavener, Oklahoma when blasting operations unearthed thirty-centimetre polished blocks which proved to be made from a type of concrete. A cave-in showed the blocks had been part of a wall which ran more than 150 metres. The fact that the wall was found in a coal seam means, in that area, it was at least 286 million years old. The obvious

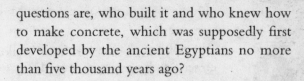

questions are, who built it and who knew how to make concrete, which was supposedly first developed by the ancient Egyptians no more than five thousand years ago?

4. Coal is formed when heat and pressure act on dead trees and vegetation over long periods of time. The oldest known coal is 390 million years old. The most recent formation dates back about two million years. The piece of coal broken open by Mrs S. W. Culp of Illinois, USA, was probably more like 65 million years old. Inside it was a perfectly preserved gold chain "of quaint and antique workmanship".

5. Coal mines have also produced a barrel-shaped block of silver, an iron pot, and a stone carved with several identical heads of an old man. All these finds are at least 260 million years old.

6. In June, 1884, a length of gold thread was found embedded in a rock from a quarry near the River Tweed. This was added to the find, forty years earlier, of a metal nail embedded in a sandstone block from Kingoodie Quarry in Scotland. Both these impossible finds are somewhere between 360 and 408 million years old.

7. An 1852 issue of the *Scientific American* described how blasting operations at Meeting

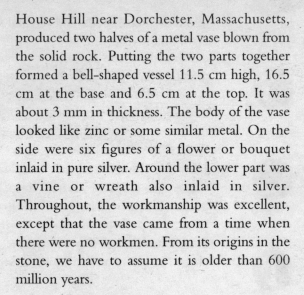

House Hill near Dorchester, Massachusetts, produced two halves of a metal vase blown from the solid rock. Putting the two parts together formed a bell-shaped vessel 11.5 cm high, 16.5 cm at the base and 6.5 cm at the top. It was about 3 mm in thickness. The body of the vase looked like zinc or some similar metal. On the side were six figures of a flower or bouquet inlaid in pure silver. Around the lower part was a vine or wreath also inlaid in silver. Throughout, the workmanship was excellent, except that the vase came from a time when there were no workmen. From its origins in the stone, we have to assume it is older than 600 million years.

8. In the summer of 1968, William J. Meister split open a block of shale near Antelope Spring, Utah, hoping to add to his fossil collection and, like Mr Reid before him, found a fossilized human shoe print. The heel was indented about 3 mm more than the sole and had the characteristic signs of wear that would mark it as a right shoe. The shale, which held trilobite remains as well as the shoe print came from Cambrian strata dated somewhere between 505 and 590 million years old.

9. A 1983 edition of the *Moscow News* reported a find in the Turkmen Republic of a fossil human footprint . . . next to the giant footprint of a three-toed dinosaur. Both prints were

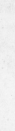

found in Jurassic rock and seemed to be about 150 million years old.

10. In 1968, archaeologists investigating fossil remnants in a chalk bed at Saint-Jean de Livet in France came upon a number of egg-shaped metal tubes. They varied in size, but were identical in shape. The chalk strata in which they were discovered dates back 65 million years. This means the tubes were dropped by somebody or something towards the end of the Cretaceous period, while the dinosaurs still ruled the earth.

• The many "impossible" finds like those listed in this Fact File have led some researchers to wonder if scientists got it right when they calculated that humanity evolved only 100,000 years ago.

• Some experts argue that odd finds in prehistoric rocks mean Earth was visited by litter louts from outer space at some stage of its long history. Most scientists, however, believe such visits are unlikely because of the vast distances involved.

Stone Me!
Weird Stone Circle Facts

Scientific research into the great stone circles and other stone monuments throughout the British Isles over the past few years has produced some very weird results. In this second of our special Fact Files, here are some of them. . .

1. On Baltinglass Hill in the Republic of Ireland, a number of prehistoric tombs are sending out radio waves. But Ireland's most famous prehistoric monument, the great mound of Newgrange, actually blanks out radio transmissions. So does one of the cairns at Loughcrew.

2. In Britain, sensitive electronic measurements have shown certain stones emit an ultrasonic click at sunrise and sunset.

3. Everywhere you go, there is a steady level of background radiation (measured with a Geiger Counter) . . . except at some stone circles where readings are higher. But if you go to sites in Cornwall, the readings are just as likely to be lower. Measurements taken in the summer of 1985 showed Geiger readings were actually halved.

4. At one Cornish circle, the Merry Maidens, measurements showed areas with above-background radiation levels, with areas below-background levels right beside them. This result is, of course, impossible.

5. A stone in the western sector of the Rollright Stones in Oxfordshire showed a rapidly changing magnetic field during a survey in 1983. Three years later it produced a visible electric "flame" which was successfully photographed by investigator Paul Devereux.

6. A retired Professor of Engineering, Alexander Thom, showed scores of stone circles throughout the British Isles were laid out in accordance with the position of the moon and may have been used as observatories. They could even be used to predict accurately the next lunar eclipse.

7. Careful measurements have shown that Stonehenge, Britain's most famous megalithic site, was laid out not only to align with certain sun and moon positions, but with underground streams and other megalithic sites as well. It seems, in fact, to be a sophisticated stone computer . . . which nobody now knows how to use.

The Incredible Plum Pudding Weirdness

Coincidences are always just a little weird. But sometimes coincidence will stretch and stretch. That's when it gets seriously weird. . .

Fifteenth-century France

The French astronomer Camille Flammarion, who died in 1925, was a widely read author, but not just on astronomy. His interests ranged from extraterrestrial life to more widespread weirdness. In 1900 he published a book called *L'Inconnu* ("The Unknown") which contained a case history that has intrigued students of coincidence ever since.

It was a story that concerned Eustache Deschamps, a fifteenth-century French poet who established rules of rhyme for French poetry still in use today. But it was not Deschamps' poetry that interested Camille Flammarion. Rather it was the man's weird gift for attracting plum pudding.

As a boy in Orléans, Deschamps was introduced to the delights of plum pudding by a Monsieur de Fortgibu, who gave him the first piece of it he had ever seen. The young Deschamps thought it was probably the finest dessert he had ever tasted. He decided he would have it whenever it was offered.

This proved a bit more difficult than he imagined. In those days, plum pudding was far more widely known in Britain than it was in France. In fact, as the young Deschamps was to discover, almost nobody else had heard of it except M. de Fortgibu.

It was fully ten years later before Deschamps had the chance to taste plum pudding again.

He had all but forgotten the exotic taste of his childhood when, dining in a Paris restaurant, he spotted plum pudding on the menu.

He could hardly finish his meal quickly enough. When the waiter arrived to take his order for dessert, he ordered a helping with fond memories of M. de Fortgibu.

Deschamps waited impatiently. In many ways he could hardly believe his luck. Although he dined out reasonably often, he had never before seen plum pudding on any French menu. And he had entered this particular restaurant for no better reason than that he was walking past it when he realized he was hungry.

But, as it turned out, his luck was out. An apologetic waiter came back moments later to say there was only one piece of plum pudding left and it had, unfortunately, already been ordered by another patron of the restaurant.

Deschamps demanded to know who had taken "his" plum pudding. The waiter told him it was Monsieur de Fortgibu.

This was quite a coincidence as it stands, but the story gets weirder.

Many years later, while attending a dinner party, Deschamps was invited by his hosts to sample a very rare but wonderful English dish – a piece of plum pudding.

Deschamps could hardly believe his ears. He told his hosts he would be delighted to try the plum pudding and explained this would be only the second time in his life he had eaten it – the first time being in childhood.

He then told the story of his experience in the restaurant and was rewarded with delighted laughter all round when he related how M. de Fortgibu had beaten him to the last piece.

Servants brought in the pudding itself and as he was being served Deschamps remarked that the only thing he needed to make the occasion complete was M. de Fortgibu.

As this point, the door burst open and an old, old man entered, obviously hopelessly lost. Deschamps stood up so quickly that his chair fell over. His mouth dropped open. The old man was Monsieur de Fortgibu.

He had been invited to another dinner altogether, had mistaken the address and burst in on the party by accident.

• The scientist Paul Kammerer was fascinated by coincidence and spent twenty years collecting examples. His interest was shared by many other well-known figures, including the physicist Wolfgang Pauli and the psychiatrist Carl Jung.

1. A Manchester couple, Jack and Mildred Corfield, flew out to Ibiza in July, 1984, only to find that their pre-booked hotel room had been given to another couple also called Jack and Mildred Corfield who had come out on the same flight. 1984 seems to have been a good year for coincidences. A month after the Corfields' holiday experience, 22-year-old Karen Dawn Southwick was married in St Michael's and All Angels Church at Tettenhall, near Wolverhampton. Three hours later another 22-year-old Karen Dawn Southwick was married in the same church. Both women were given away by their fathers, both of whom were called Alfred Southwick.

2. In November, 1910, an Austrian gentleman went to a concert where he had seat number 9 and cloakroom ticket number 9. The following evening, at another concert, he had seat number 21 and cloakroom ticket number 21.

3. Jung's patients sometimes suffered from coincidence as well. The wife of one of them, who thought he was with Jung, rang Jung and asked if her husband was all right. Jung told her he had just left, but he was fine. But the wife was still worried. When her grandfather died, a flock of birds had come to the window of his bedroom. The same thing happened when her father died. Now, she said, a flock of birds had come to her husband's bedroom window and she was sure he had died. She was right. He died of a heart attack soon after leaving Jung's consulting room . . . at the time the birds came to his window.

4. In October, 1979, a man named Smart Ngwenya was brought into Bulawayo Magistrates Court to answer charges of tampering with a motor car. He denied the charge before Court officials realized they had brought in the wrong man. Even though his name was also Smart Ngwenya, he had come to Court purely to give evidence in another case. The wrong Smart Ngwenya was released with an apology and Court officials went off to find the right one. Minutes later they brought in Smart Ngwenya who also denied the charge and turned out to be the wrong man too, despite having the identical name. On the third attempt, the right Smart Ngwenya was found and brought to Court.

5. Thirteen-year-old Roger Lausier was swimming near the beach at Salem, Massachusetts, in 1974, when he heard a woman calling that her husband was drowning. Roger, himself a strong swimmer, saw that the man had fallen from a motor boat and was in obvious difficulty. Roger grabbed an inflatable raft, swam over and managed to keep the man afloat until a rescue boat arrived. When he was presented with an award by the Massachusetts Humane Society, Roger discovered the man he had rescued was the husband of the woman who had saved Roger from drowning nine years previously on the same beach.

The Boy from Nowhere

Sometimes you'd almost think there were holes in space. People and things disappear into nowhere or appear from nowhere. And none more mysteriously than Kaspar Hauser. . .

Nuremberg, Germany, 26 May, 1828

A cobbler named George Weichmann was crossing Unschlitt Square in Nuremberg when he saw an odd-looking figure approach down the hill. It was a boy of about seventeen, well-built, but dressed in rags and walking stiff-legged.

The boy looked healthy. His boots were too small, but his shirt, breeches, hat and jacket were all far too large. As he approached Weichmann, he held out an envelope addressed to the Captain of the 4th Squadron, 6th Cavalry Regiment in Nuremberg.

Weichmann took the boy to the nearest military post, from where he was taken to the home of Captain Wessenig, the commander of the 4th Squadron.

By the time Wessenig got home, the place was in an uproar. The boy had tried to pick up a candle-flame with his fingers. He had failed to recognize ham and beer, but wolfed down black bread and water. The smell of cooking made him ill, he was frightened by the ticking of a clock and he answered every question with "Weiss nicht" ("I don't know").

There were two unsigned letters in the envelope he carried. One, dated October 1812, seemed to have been written by the boy's mother. She named him only as Kaspar, said he was born on 30 April 1812, and claimed his father was a soldier.

The second letter was written in a different hand. It came from a labourer who said Kaspar's mother had asked him to bring up the boy. He had, he said, never let Kaspar out of the house except at night.

All this seemed clear enough – a young girl, unable to bring up her child, abandons him in what she believes to be a good home and the man of the house eventually passes him on to the Army. The problem was Kaspar himself.

Kaspar knew the word for "horse" and could parrot, "I want to be a cavalryman like my father" but could say little else. There was also the mystery of his odd behaviour – he had obviously never before seen a candle-flame and point blank refused to eat anything but bread and water. Captain Wessenig took him to the police.

In the police station, Kaspar was asked to write his name and address. He laboriously wrote Kaspar Hauser, but was unable to give an address. The police searched him. He was carrying a rosary, a packet of salt and two religious tracts. His feet were soft and badly blistered from walking.

The police then got to work on the letters and discovered they were fakes, recently written by the same person. With no further clues, they locked Kaspar in a cell for observation.

Kaspar sat absolutely immobile for hours on end. He could see in the dark and obviously preferred darkness to light. He knew nothing of things like clocks or coins or knives. He had one word for all animals ("horse") and could not tell the difference between men and women, both of whom he called "boy". He had no sense of time.

Despite this unhappy start, Kaspar Hauser quickly learned to talk properly, to write and to cope with everyday objects. Six weeks after he was discovered, the Burgermeister and Council of Nuremberg issued a statement that described the boy's early life as he was now able to explain it.

Kaspar said he had lived in a small, dark cell. The only window was boarded up, the only furnishing was a pile of straw. He could either sit or lie, but not stand. He slept on the straw and each time he awoke there was a loaf of dark bread and a jug of water by his side.

From time to time, the water would be drugged. He would fall into a deep sleep and wake up to find his clothing changed, his hair and nails cut. He lived in the cell for as long as he could remember.

One day, the statement continued, a big, brawny man let himself into Kaspar's cell, gave him a board to lean on, a sheet of paper and a pencil, then taught him how to write the name KASPAR HAUSER in block capitals. He also taught him the words "horse", "I want to be a soldier like my father" and "I don't know".

The day came when Kaspar woke from his drugged sleep to find he was wearing boots. The man came in and took him out of his cell. Kaspar felt dizzy in the open air. His feet hurt when he walked. The man came with him for a distance, but Kaspar entered Nuremberg alone.

If Kaspar Hauser's beginnings were odd, his end was positively weird. He died on 17 December, 1833. The cause of death was a stab wound sustained three days before. He claimed to have been stabbed by a tall, cloaked man in the public park of Ansbach, a town near Nuremberg. He insisted the man handed him a purse before stabbing him. But Kaspar did not know who the man was, or where he came from.

The purse handed to Kaspar by his murderer contained a note in mirror writing which read:

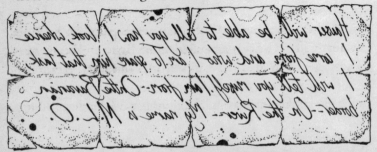

(Hauser will be able to tell you how I look, whence I come from and who I am. To spare him that task, I will tell you myself. I am from – On the Bavarian border – On the River – My name is M.L.O.)

Captain Hickel, who investigated the scene of the stabbing, claimed the only set of footprints in the area was Kaspar's own, yet the purse Kaspar claimed to have been given was actually found.

Nobody ever discovered where Kaspar came from. Nobody ever found the man who murdered him – the man who left no footprints. Kaspar's own story about the years of confinement in a cell on bread and water was obviously nonsense. But why did he lie? And where did he really come from?

• There are lots of problems with the story Kaspar told to the authorities. He was a burly lad of about seventeen when he was found, yet showed no signs of malnutrition despite his supposedly lengthy diet of bread and water. For someone who had spent seventeen years in the dark, he somehow managed not to be completely blinded by sunlight. And he could walk immediately after being let out of a tiny cell where he claimed he had no exercise for years.

• At the same time, Kaspar *could* see in the dark. He *did* find sunlight painful and his feet were tender and blistered as if he was unaccustomed to walking.

• The authorities mounted a nation–wide search for his jailer, or anyone else who might shed some light on the mystery. They failed to find anything, even after offering a reward.

• Three centuries before the mysterious death of Kaspar

Hauser, another man made a habit of mirror writing like the note Kaspar's murderer gave him – the great artistic genius, Leonardo da Vinci. No one has ever explained this peculiarity. Leonardo's extensive notebooks were fluently hand written *backwards*. You need to hold them up to a mirror to read them.

• Many physicists now believe the cosmos is made up of many parallel universes. One physicist, Dr Fred Allen Wolf, thinks we live at the centre of mirror images of our past and future stretching to infinity. If we could enter one of these reflections, like Alice climbing through the looking-glass, we could, for all practical purposes travel in time. And if we climbed back again, we might bring with us a tendency to mirror writing.

1. On 24 October, 1593, a Spanish soldier reported for guard duty at the palace in Mexico City. He seemed unhappy and confused and his uniform, while obviously military, was not that of the palace guards.

He was hauled away for interrogation and quickly admitted he was not sure where he was. He thought he had somehow lost his way while walking to the palace. But it soon turned out the palace he was looking for was not in Mexico City. He had been ordered to report for duty at the palace of Manila on the Philippines.

The interrogators could make no sense of it, but worse was to come. The man insisted he had been stationed in Manila and had received his orders there that very morning. In the days of sailing ships, the fastest journey from Manila to Mexico took months.

The man could not possibly be telling the truth, but he seemed determined to add detail upon detail to his story. He mentioned, for example, that the Spanish Governor of the Philippines had been killed the night before.

When they told him he was now in South America, he looked amazed. Since they assumed he was lying, the military authorities locked him up.

He remained locked up for two months. Then a ship from the Philippines confirmed that the Governor was indeed dead – murdered on the night before the soldier turned up so mysteriously in Mexico.

The man was released and returned to Manila . . . where it was confirmed he had disappeared on the same day he turned up in Mexico.

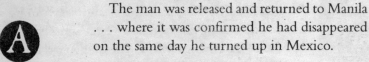

2. The Devil's Sea, situated off Japan's eastern coast and sometimes known as the Dragon's Triangle, seems to contain a hole in space which swallows ships and planes at an alarming rate.

From 1968 to 1972 the Triangle officially claimed 1,472 small ships. The official tally of major ships lost in the area since 1949 is forty. In March of 1957 it claimed three planes within two weeks.

Many of these losses have perfectly reasonable explanations but others defy logic. Between 1949 and 1954 ten large ships vanished, taking hundreds of crewmen with them and leaving no trace whatsoever. In 1942 an Imperial Japanese Navy task force, consisting of three destroyers and two aircraft carriers, mysteriously disappeared. There is no Allied report indicating these vessels were lost to enemy action.

A radio transmission from Zero F Wing Commander Shiro Kawamoto crossing the Triangle near the end of the war in 1945 may cast some light on the mystery. The last thing he said was, ". . . something is happening in the sky . . . the sky is opening up—"

3. In June, 1871, a twenty-eight metre long

riverboat called the *Iron Mountain* steamed out of Vicksburg, USA, towing two barges. She carried fifty-five passengers and crew and a cargo of molasses. Two hours later another boat found the barges adrift, the tow lines cut cleanly halfway along the length of rope. The *Iron Mountain* left no debris and no trace of its passengers, crew or cargo.

4. In January, 1989, Graham Marden, a Dorset businessman, drove into the Rownhams Service station on the M27 near Southampton. He filled up, paid his bill and asked directions to the loo. But having stepped in to the washroom, he never came out. After a while, with Marden's car blocking the pumps, the cashier knocked on the door, then used his master key to open up. The room was empty. Police arrived shortly afterwards and searched the area with tracker dogs. They found nothing.

5. Benjamin Bathurst, British consul to the Court of Emperor Francis in Vienna was in the small German town of Perleberg on 25 November, 1809, examining a team of horses. His valet and secretary both watched him walk around to the other side of the horses . . . where he vanished.

6. In AD 117 a whole Roman Legion went the same way. The tough, battle-hardened IX Hispania Legion was stationed in Britain. The soldiers marched north to fight the Picts. Four thousand men of the Legion passed through the tiny village of Dunblane in Scotland . . . and disappeared. The Picts claimed no victory. Indeed, there is no record of any battle. There were no dispatches from the Legion and relief columns found no one anywhere who had seen anything of the Romans after Dunblane.

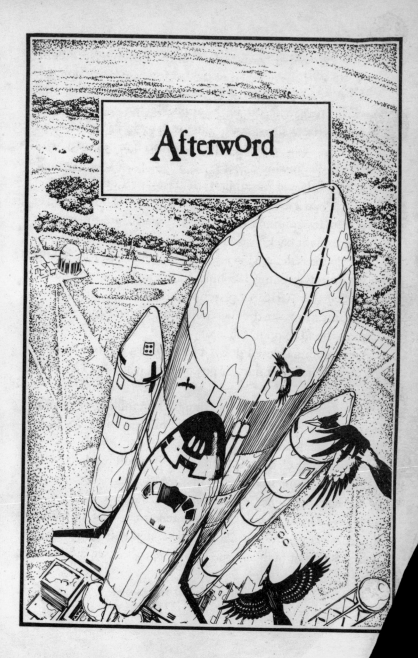

Afterword

The trouble with this sort of stuff is that you go nuts trying to figure out why it happens.

It's easy enough to see why John Ofosu of Ghana dressed fourteen pregnant goats in T-shirts. He was trying to steal them at the time and thought disguises might be useful.

But how do you explain the character in Uganda who dresses gorillas in clown suits?

Is there a deeper meaning to the fact that a dog warden in Bristol was bitten in the neck, arms and legs in 1993 . . . by people?

As humans continue to pollute the world, are the animals starting to fight back?

Woodpeckers delayed the July 1995 launch of the Space Shuttle for six days by pecking 135 holes in the fuel tank insulation.

A South African porcupine cut off telephone communications in the Vereeniging district by chewing through the fibre optic cables.

Ants in China closed down a factory, blacked out an hotel and were attacking a nuclear power plant when last I heard of them in 1995.

But then people do strange things. Two million of them in Japan have joined a religion that compels them to laugh during funerals and natural disasters.

Somebody called R. S. Robot was elected President of the Indonesian Computer Society in 1986.

At the Invention Convention in Pasadena, California, in 1993, Nelson E. Camus demonstrated a new type of battery that runs on pee. When filled, it generated enough power to light a 100-watt bulb and run both a television set and stereo.

Why all this weirdness?

If you've any ideas, you might let me know.